THE GOLDEN Touch

Nicolas Brasch
Amanda Dawson

Rigby

www.Rigby.com
1-800-531-5015

Rigby Focus Forward

This Edition © 2009 Rigby, a Harcourt Education Imprint

Published in 2007 by Nelson Australia Pty Ltd ACN: 058 280 149
A Cengage Learning company

1 2 3 4 5 6 7 8 374 14 13 12 11 10 09 08 07
Printed and bound in China

The Golden Touch
ISBN-13   978-1-4190-3755-9
ISBN-10   1-4190-3755-2

THE Golden Touch

Nicolas Brasch
Amanda Dawson

Contents

Chapter 1

King of a Large Land

A long, long time ago,
there lived a king.

His name was King Midas,
and he ruled over a large land.

He was a good king,
much loved by his people,
but he had one downfall.

4

He knew that other kings had
far more money than he did,
and he wished that he was
as rich as they were.

One day, King Midas was walking
through his palace garden
when he saw a man asleep
in a flower bed.

King Midas woke the man and asked,
"What are you
doing here?"

The man got a shock.

He had never met the king before,
and he knew that he was in big trouble.

"I have no money for food or shelter,"
the man told the king.
"I have nowhere else to go."

Chapter 2

An Act of Kindness

King Midas took pity on the man
and took him back to the palace.

There he made sure that the man had
lots of food and drink.
He also gave him a warm bed
to sleep in for ten days.

At the end of the ten days,
King Midas gave the man some money
and sent him on his way.

The man was very grateful.

Watching over this act of kindness
was Dionysus, one of the gods.

Dionysus appeared before King Midas
and said, "I want to reward your kind act.
I grant you one wish."

King Midas saw that, finally,
he had a chance to be richer than
all the other kings he knew.

"I want everything I touch
to turn to gold," he told Dionysus.

"I'm not sure that's such a good idea,"
Dionysus said.
"Are you sure you don't want
something else?"

"No, that's what I want," King Midas said.

So Dionysus granted King Midas
his wish.

Chapter 3

The Golden Touch

King Midas decided to try out
his new power.
He reached down and picked up a rock.
It turned to gold.

He picked a flower,
and it turned to gold, too.

"This is fantastic!"
King Midas said to himself.

At dinner time, King Midas sat
in front of a huge feast.
His excitement had made him
very hungry.
But as he picked up a chicken leg,
it turned to gold.
He could not eat it.

Then he grabbed a bunch of grapes,
and it turned to gold, too.

King Midas called for his daughter.
When she arrived, he said,
"Please feed me or I will starve."

The king's daughter picked up a fig
and put it in the king's mouth.
As he ate the fig, he touched
his daughter's hand.
She turned to gold.

"Oh, no!" he screamed.
"What have I done?"

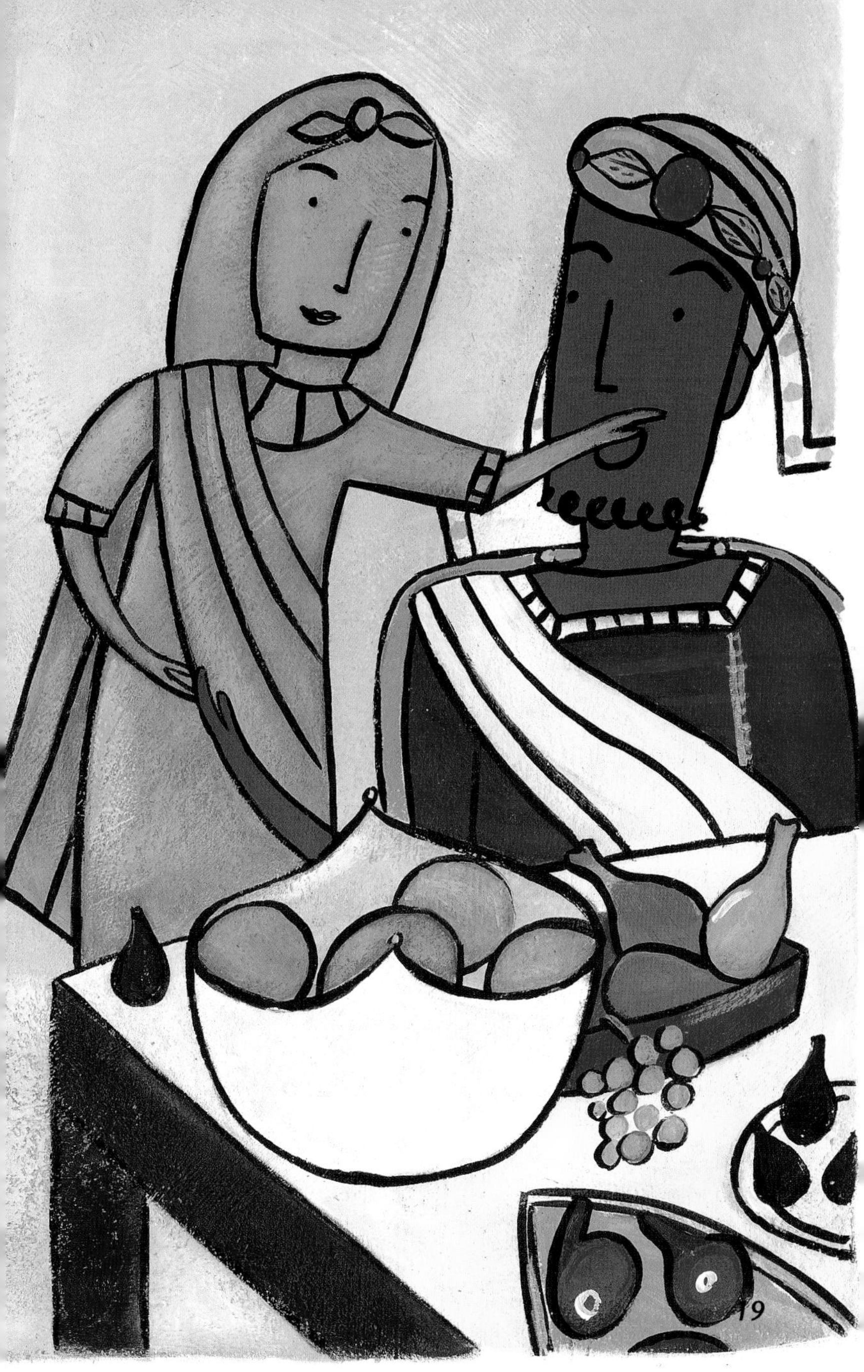

Chapter 4

Happily Ever After

King Midas called out to Dionysus.
Dionysus appeared before him again.

"Please remove my wish!"
pleaded the King.
"I was so greedy, and now I am
so unhappy."

"I can remove your wish,"
Dionysus told him.
"But if I do, you will be poorer
than you were before."

"That's fine," said King Midas.
"Please do it now."

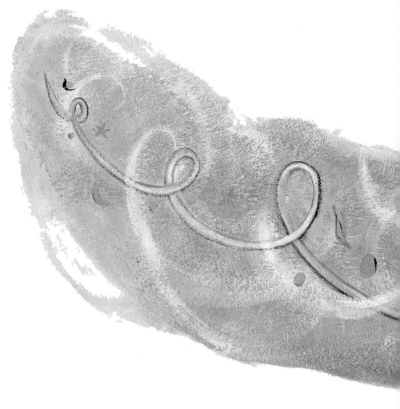

Dionysus removed the wish.

King Midas was poorer than
he had ever been before,
but he was much happier as well.

Unlike many kings,
he now knew that there were far more
important things than money.